Windmills and Bridges

POEMS NEAR AND FAR

Susan Ford Wiltshire

EAKIN PRESS Austin, Texas

for Matthew and Carrie

poets

Cover design by Jamie Adams.
Cover photograph by Ashley T. Wiltshire, Jr.

For CIP information, please access: www.loc.gov

FIRST EDITION

Published in the United States of America
By Eakin Press
A Division of Sunbelt Media, Inc.
P.O. Drawer 90159 Austin, Texas 78709-0159
email: sales@eakinpress.com
website: www.eakinpress.com

1 2 3 4 5 6 7 8 9
1-57168-639-8

CONTENTS

Bridges

Preface

In June 1541, the conquistador Coronado, searching for gold, passed across the vast treeless prairie of what would become, nearly three centuries later, the Panhandle of Texas. Parts of ten counties of the Llano Estacado, the Staked Plains, were traded in the late 1870s to a Chicago syndicate in exchange for building a state capitol in Austin. That was the origin of the XIT Ranch—Ten in Texas—which in time was sold piecemeal to settlers coming into the state.

On that land I was born.
There was no water.
Windmills, going deep, made it possible
    to live there.
Bridges, mostly of the mind,
    gave the world to inhabit.

Windmills

TRANSLATION

At night the sounds of a windmill
sidle up as company against
the ceaseless assail
of the wind:

kindly clunks, not quite melodic,
of galvanized sheet metal fans
and tail fin catching the wind
as they bend;

sturdy thumps every twenty seconds or so
as check balls plunk into reverse
to lift life four hundred feet
to our need.

PLANTING IRIS

I loved iris for years before I planted any,
then a hundred over a week or more
one September when I was fifty-five.

As I dug I puzzled over where I got it from,
why it was iris I wanted to plant
more than any other thing I might have done,

could think of no one in my family
who cared for flowers anyway
except one great-grandmother
who died the day that I turned five.

When the work was done I called my mother,
told her of the planting. She said
Not a spring went by that your father
did not say he wished he had
planted iris the fall before.

So then I knew, one tiny piece I had
not known, never heard him say it,
but knew it true in the marrow of my bone.

Bone? Is the love of iris buried deep
there too in some baffling dance
of those gyring spirals of DNA?

If I could know only one lettered
sequence of the four nucleotides
of one gene of one chromosome
of those twenty-three resolute pairs
that cast me upon the shore
as who I thought I only was,

what more might I yet learn
of the abyss that is the father
I deigned to think I knew
but did not know loved iris?

MEO FILIO

Aetat 1

after Catullus

Ludis ut passer volitans circum nunc
gremium meum, fortiter, libenter.
Cum tandem te emittere erit necesse,
tum precor ut sim, similis te, fili,
    libera et fortis.

You play now like a sparrow
flying around my breast, bravely, freely.
When at last it will be necessary to let you go,
I pray that I may be like you, child,
    Free and brave.

HARVEST IN THE BARN

Come end of June
the harvest if there is one
is in the barn.

And so it was
when our dear fledgling
returned to roost
before her next flight out.

We passed our days in such delight
it could have broke my heart
had not all been so gentle
and so right.

Still I,
who know of hail and drought,
doubted whether I deserved
to have my harvest in the barn
at all, and all the more
when I surveyed my neighbors' fields
and saw their crops
at risk of being lost
as ours so nearly was.

Then I recalled that harvests
are not for barns
but for the hungry.
Barns are only for safekeeping
for the passing through.

Then I knew
the answer to my doubt,
and my brief flirt with guilt
gave way to summer
savored to the hilt.

SCISSORED

On her final college holiday
our daughter, latter-born of two,
prepared furiously through the night
for her first job interview.

I circled in her radius.
Why are you staying up? she asked.
You're supporting me, aren't you?
Of course, I said. I was, of course.

At the airport door she walked straight
through without a backward glance.
We watched her disappear into the crowd,
turned to one another in wonderment.

I felt scissored, as surely as
our firstborn's start at kindergarten,
when I wandered blindly by the office to see
if they had any counseling for me.

This departure was the final one.
The last one's leaving meant
that both had left forever
the safe familiar of our world.

For them this is continuum, their worlds
circling larger while still including ours.
For me, it was completion, a gate
I traversed at the far end of a field

I tended for over twenty years—
breaking, tilling, planting, cultivating,
weeding, protecting, fending off
the terrifying pass of storms.

What those dear two do not know is that
I too begin new voyages to far lands
of mind and spirit. Only a simulacrum mom
waits hopefully home by the phone.

I pause at the gate, waft a prayer
of gratitude for the harvested field behind,
take measure of the trackless plain ahead,
and slowly start the crossing.

VIGIL

I wanted to know
how baby birds leave the nest.
Do they fall first,
then fly from the ground?

Are they pushed out by their mother?
Do all fly at once?
What time of day do they leave?
How do they know when to go?

(If you have seen how this happens,
skip over this poem and go to the next.)

* * * * * *

Small black birds like swallows
build nests on our porch every season.
Each year I count eggs, know when they hatch,
hope always to catch them ready to fly.

Always before I found only their leavings.
This year four young were still in the nest
and I had long summer days to invest.

Here's what I saw in my vigil:

Birds sleep at night as we do,
so I watched only by day.
Mothers feed themselves first,
I noted intently. Nestling breakfast
begins about quarter to six. Mouths gape.

At first that was all the babes could do,
chirp and gape. Then they started
flexing their wings in the nest,
circling their tails over the side.

That was their first independence,
going to the bathroom alone.
(I should have known.)
If the mother was swooping by at the time,
she caught the poop neatly and took it away.

Sometimes she caught a piece in midair.
She did not seem to care what fell below,
but the nest itself she always kept clean.
This caretaking filled all her day.

For two days I watched, never bored.
Sometimes the fledglings huddled primly
like penguins. Mostly they chittered,
especially as mother approached with a bite.

More and more they seemed to be practicing:
Sometimes they perched on nestside
facing in, holding on for dear life, whirring
their wings in a blur fast as hummingbirds.
What caused them to know how to go?
No nestlings nearby cajoled them
to come out and play, taunting them
like teenagers to flee from their home.

Finally, on the third afternoon,
one flew out on his own, flapped wildly
toward the opposite wall, hit the ceiling,
returned to the ledge alongside the nest.

Three beaks pivot toward him. Mother
feeds him outside of the nest. A second
flutters out for a visit, then retreats.
Mother feeds the three still in the nest.

Sometimes she chooses, sometimes she
feeds the first one who begs.
Suddenly all goes quiet. Are they resting?
Is the cat out? Is other danger nearby?

Then it happened: Three of them flew away
almost at once, bounced off the low ceiling,
got their bearings, whirled to a nearby tree.

One stayed behind, seemingly without dismay.
After a while he looked around,
hopped onto the edge of the nest,
sailed off, hit the ceiling,
swooped under the roof and onto a tree.

This I saw.

I have heard this:
fledglings their first night out
of the nest huddle together
on a branch for warmth.

I hope it is true.

ALCHEMY

tene plumbum, aurum sequeter
Hold on to the lead, the gold will follow

Newton studied alchemy for years
because he believed that God acts
in every element of the universe
so even lead can change to gold.

Four centuries later, Vladimir Haensel
added platinum to fossil fuel.
All was gain: higher octane without the lead,
raw materials for plastics remained.

On a day he was honored,
Haensel spoke of the power of catalysis,
how bodies loosen, break down, reform,
old always turning into new.

Listening rapt, she thought of writers:
If they follow faithfully enough
the practice of pencil upon the page,
their lead too may turn to gold.

TWO VERSIONS OF ONE STORY

The Gift

From the folds
of time's garment
shrouded by seven
decades of oblivion
appeared a tiny book of poems,
Mother, by Edwin Markham,
inscribed by my father,
twenty-two that year,
to his "darling mother,
Valentine's Day, 1926,"
a twenty-dollar bill
still pressed primly
between aging pages
crisp with disuse.

No trifle this, I guessed,
but testament, a balm
in the Gilead of tears,
preserved first by resolution,
then by years.

I first imagined that Lura chose
to savor and save these gifts
from her sole surviving child
(her first son dead at eighteen months,
seven years before this one was born,
now her husband newly dead
too soon two years ago),
against a day when

young Frank would fail
to call or bring a gift at all—
the Depression coming on.

Depression

Later I wondered
if my father's mother
ever saw the bill,
if she laid the book
aside unopened,
one more useless proof
of the impotence
of all the world's bids
to change her rage
against her fate—
a depression coming on.

MRS. WILSON

"You want to be immortal?"
asked the preacher at Easter.
"Love somebody."

Mrs. Wilson, having known exclusion,
knew to take in the exiled.
So she took care of "her boys"
in the rebirthplace of democracy,
the nation's capital,
in the zip code that meant no life insurance,
heinous mark of Cain.

She was mother to orphans
whose own had disowned them—
caring, cleaning, loving,
sharing the beloved spaniel Mrs. B.

Best of all, she was hospitality.
With her they did not have to
hide the dailiness
of their lives together.

They loved her back before they died.
One did more:
He was her friend.
He went to her home in the projects,
along the train line to Philadelphia
where she had raised her own children well.

Having no time or money,
he gave her both
on a deep winter day.

She died at Easter.
Some fine Easter he would too.
No matter.
They are forever.

FOR JOHN

> Even in our sleep, pain we cannot
>   forget falls
> drop by drop upon the heart,
>   until, in our
> despair, against our will, comes
>   wisdom through the
> awful grace of God.
>
> —Aeschylus

Leaving, I grieve
the limits of love,
that I cannot build a bulwark against
the sliding places of your life.

No, I am wrong.
To wish that
is to deny your power
to do it for yourself
or to presume that I could know
the landscape of your need.

Instead I reach out like a girder
over the traffic of our lives
to connect with you
tighten the bolts
and build together a brace sufficient against
any wind.

SPLIT DECISION

There is no shield in the Gulf storm
for that child first time out of Kentucky.

The only thing shrinking about our friend's
lymphoma is the hopes of her friends.

The world's sorrows eclipse mine,
my brother said as he called to tell me his,

citing the boys and girls in the desert
and the young mother's cancer,

but grieving the loss
of a place to love and to die.

Comparing sorrows commits violence
against the sorrowing, I know,

but he is my near brother, so
I, only sister, will reach

out to share the sorrows of others,
in to share his.

EASTER POEM II

I promised you
we would build a girder
across our lives
sufficient against any wind.

But how could I know then
that you would become the wind?
Powerful even when still,
moved by forces you may know now,
not the callow fripperies
of some eddying breeze
but the inexorable tide
of the Panhandle sky.

Or are you altogether gone
who always loved to wander?
Did you follow the sound
of the outward bound
one last time,
a mariner off to the stars?

But if you are altogether gone,
why am I sometimes bent to the ground,
hapless as wheat against
a blue Texas norther?

Why do I sometimes howl at the moon
like a coyote in the scant hiatus of
dead calm before dusk?

Why, in these still hollows of Tennessee,
have I come to feel most at home
when a strong wind blows?

Why, at last, in my sad loss,
against my will, do I begin to sense
sometimes almost as a blessing
the wind at my back?

LINES WRITTEN IN A WAITING ROOM, MAD, SO AS NOT TO BE SO MUCH SO

He left the room
in surly silence,
the one for whom
our fabricated hopes
surpassed the scope he knows.

His wordlessness revealed
a wound, his own,
that has not healed—
and left behind,
once more,
the dying brother as the
liveliest in the room.

What is there to do
but salute the departing,
pray for the maimed,
and dance all the way
to the door?

REVERSE SAMARITAN

On rare roads
the most generous act
possible toward a person
who causes hurt by habit
is to pass kindly by,
depositing at the inn
not the wounded wounder
but the tiresome tedium
of one's own righteousness.

ARCHAEOLOGY OF THE HEART

An Alzheimer's Story

A brain confettied by Alzheimer's
contains pockets of consciousness
cast off like detritus from the cosmology
of circuits keeping a person whole.

Third-born of three, Sarah knew from childhood
she was a "mistake," not cherished by a mother
who made clear to all her preference for boys.
(How Sarah knew all this I grieve to guess.)

I am not unlucky in my mother-in-law.
She never was unkind to me.
These days, though, when visitors come,
she is warm and courteous to everyone.

She nursed her parents, husband, then his parents
to their deaths. Now it is our turn to care for her.

Strange transformation:
In the autumn of this dread disease
she cares for others when they come.

On a recent visit I found Sarah in her wheelchair
    in the hall.
How did you know just when to come? she asked.
I need some care today. I am trying to decide what
    I want.
She asked me how I decide what it is I want.

Those who care for people with Alzheimer's practice
constantly the art of improvisation. I temporized:
Yes, it's hard to know what you want.
Let's find a pleasant place to talk about it.

What was troubling her? Why this distress?
Why this question now that I had never heard
her ask,
doubted if she had ever asked before,
perhaps even of herself.

In a comfortable corner looking out on a sunny day
she spoke of the kind of house she wanted.
This place isn't right, she said with a sidewise
glance.
But how do you know what you want?

Sometimes you have to know yourself well,
I ventured. What do you want most of all?
A house with parents, she said, and a regular
family.

Of course, I thought, her childhood home in
Virginia.
You mean like the house on Barton Avenue?
I prompted.
I was wrong. No, she corrected, the house on
Perkins.
Now she was digging into a deep unknown to me.
I imagined she had once been happy there.

I persisted: What about the house you and
Ashley Sr.
built on Hermitage Road?—their family home for
forty years.
Oh, we never bought that house, she said.
We only rented it on a trial basis.

I nodded, took a different tack.
How was it for you growing up with your family?
I asked. How was it with your brother Russell?
She said, He was a . . . big brother. It was okay.

And with your sister? I dared ask, more cautious.
That was harder. She said, She was smarter in the
books
than I was. Margaret and Russell both were.
They both moved up.

There. She had said it, exposed at last to the light
the pain that had weighed her all her life.

Archaeologists dig through many layers of debris
to reach the foundation of a dwelling place.
On one shiny afternoon Alzheimer's permitted
one of its initiates to dig deep through the
disintegration of almost a lifetime to reach
a house with a regular family on Perkins Street
where once lived a child who was happy.

HIEROGLYPH

Burdened by a list of duties
she dreaded doing,
she decided instead
to translate tasks
into hieroglyphs,
summoning mysteries
into pictures of
the thing contained.

These depictions
formed upon her page:
The privilege of stewardship;
A gift for a friend;
Music for stirring the day;
Time with a wise ally;
Sharing a book that mattered;
Making something new.

This holy script
transformed
the dun of duty
into the compass of love.

ABECEDARIUM

Avoid abstractions
Be creative
Care calmly
Dare defeat
Enjoy children
Fear not at all
Get up early
Hold on
Invest in the impossible
Judge sparingly
Know solitude
Love laughter
Make big mistakes only once
Need knowingly
Organize
Practice politics
Quit worrying
Risk writing
Sin bravely
Trust God more bravely
Understand
Venture far
Walk or run
XV miles every week, and let
Youth be less
Zealous than age.

POSITIVE

Think positive, chirped the worker
at the gym as I left for the good day
I was instructed also to have.

How, I thought, in her innocence
could she presume to fit the same advice
to every stranger she salutes?

At the moment I passed her by
I was plumbing the murk, dead set
on making sense of some unopinioned dark.

For an instant I was enticed to hoist
my sail wide and white as a smile,
set to scud breezily into the day.

But, being peculiarly curious,
I held instead to the work of discerning
what is below the surface I traverse

so when I arrive at the other side
I'll know the whole of where I've been,
the reefs as well as the gleamy sea.

Bridges

SIBLING SONG*

Our oldest story holds Cain against Abel.
Being brother or sister
to sister or brother is laden with danger.

Joseph's brothers could not bear their father's
favor toward his lastborn fair, so sold him
into slavery for his Lakers coat.

Hector's fool of a brother caused much trouble
for Troy
by choosing Aphrodite who beguiled him with
promises of another man's wife
if he would judge her fairest of her female kin
who themselves were competing for the
age-old prize of prettiest.

Wolf-suckled Romulus slew his twin for the rule
of Rome.
The warring brothers of Thebes killed each other
in one sally of spears at the walls of home.

Are we all chained to Cain in this script with
no sense?
If God made the choice that caused Cain's despite,
why did innocent Abel die?

Would siblings compete with no prizes to gain?
Are they so fearful of offending a father
they inflict their rage on each other?

* * * * * *

---

*in memory of Dietrich Bonhoeffer, February 4, 1906–April 9, 1945, and Sabine Bonhoeffer Leibholz, February 4, 1906–July 7, 1999

It is not always so, does not have to be.
Two at least were linked in soul from
the moment he arrived, then she—

sooner, perhaps, if their two hearts beat out
a frail tattoo in unison in their cocoon's
dark swelling sea.

She said the union between them was different
in kind from their relations
with the other six:

If one were hungry or hurt, the other knew.
They never were on opposite sides.
They were a team, she said.

Each night they fixed their minds upon eternity
(the pact between them no other guessed),
each vying to bid the last goodnight.

In their family of scientists, she heard him ask:
Does God sit down to lunch each day?
Does God love chimney sweeps?

When she chose a mate, he embraced him too,
became his friend, helped both escape
when lawless bans imperiled them.

He made his own way, theologian, man for others,
found another who shared his great faith,
cornflowers free by the fields.

At the end he yet said yes to life, tutored from
the womb
by the sister who survived him half a century,
whole and fine—wife, mother, friend—

but for all her days in unanticipated moments felt
half her heart constrict with missing him
like an amputated limb.

FIRST DAY OUT ON A LONG JOURNEY

Leaning to walk for the first time
up the swaying gangway of a strange ship
with new mates or old made odd
in the absence of all familiar,

no hooks for hanging expectation on,
a failure of nerve descends.
Back-home anticipations, so etched and eager,
clinging to doorposts like a joyless child

in time are shaken away like water from a spaniel
pointing with determination
toward a horizon as unmarked
and receding as the sea.

Finally one laughs at all that is left behind,
turns to stride into the unknown
that will become familiar when tamed
by habit and time and delight.

NO FREE VERSE

On Arriving in Nauplion Not Knowing How to Spend the Day

Would it be better to sit
in Syntagma all day,
pen poised to play,
books stacked at hand?

Or better to follow the organized plan
board the bus see the sites
do what is right
if not what I choose?

What I choose to pursue
is the gleam in my eye
the dream on the fly
a story to spin.

But I can only write out of where I've been.
Each word bears the cost
of another one lost.
For every line my words cause to grow

there's another missed where I did not go.
One poem lays waste to another:
while writing one, one loses the other.
There is a price to a poem.

TETHERED

in the Sahara

Donkeys in the desert inch forward
like lumpish slugs or aged crones,
forefeet hobbled by rags.

A milk cow, ribbed and scrawny-haunched,
seeks scant graze along the
radius of her rope.

One misstep and each could die. And I?
Bound close as heart to heart
to my certain ones,

tethered by varying lengths of loyalty
to friends and loves and place
and work and cause,

I gaze out from the ends of all my ropes
toward glistening distances
quick as a fennec,

gliding as gulls savoring their fill,
but freer than either because
of something I know.

SECOND HARVEST

No one follows where machines
reap wheat. Their sweep is clean.
But where terrain or need
require the scythe,
two harvests happen.

Owners send their minions
through the fields
to load their caravans
for the port before hurrying
to the adjoining field
to reap its profit too.

Evening creeps,
and second harvesters arrive,
women gleaning what others
left behind upon the ground
or close against high weeds.

One knows the need
of more than food.
Her staple crop is stories.
She works in stealth,
taking only leavings
no one else would see
or need or claim to own.

These she will glean,
grind, mix, knead,
let rise with the yeast of words.
These loaves distributed,
her granary is restored.

FORMATION

The apparitions rise in clumps
along the horizon,
begin inching forward,
form into ranks like geese,
scatter rapidly,
reverse, gather again,
and finally glide to a landing
where she waits.

They disappear from sight.
Soon they are as busy
in her brain as Pompeiian cupids
focused on their appointed tasks.

She waits intently,
lends a hand where she can.
In time, astounded, she watches them
stride in contented cadence
down her arm to take
their necessary places
precisely on the page.

ST. GREGORY'S HOLE
Aghia Sophia, Istanbul

A marble column soars, improbably pierced
by a thumb-size hole, stamen of a penumbral
floret twice the radius of a human hand.

A wish comes true, they say, if with the thumb
as center-pin one can inscribe a full circuit
on the stone with fingers spreading like a clock.

She stood aloof with condescending smile
as eager applicants strained in queue
to gain their wishes through their thumbs

Until with a start she saw that she too is a column
smudged by nearly sixty years of learning
how much harder than wishing choosing is.

JANISSARY / HAREM
Topkapi Palace

It is permitted to convert
a child, said the guide.
An adult must agree.

The female daughter,
the one over whom hangs
beauty or a parent's greed,
is sold to the harem,
abased for one fleet lust
like daughters still
until the caged bird sings
or the caged bird dies.

Her ten-year-old brother
joins the janissaries
or the gang or platoon
where all one has to take
or give is one's life.
Is he any freer than the girl-child
confined in rooms built so
doors and windows face only in?

How fragile the chance
for any male child or girl
to grow free and strong
into that good thing:

An adult who can choose to agree.

RETURNING, REVISED

The lapping waters laughed
when the master returned home at last
from gleaming Asia to gentle Sirmio.

But it was not the same Catullus
who came home to those familiar shores
and longed-for kiss of sheets—

says one who wrestles upon return
with how to take up the threads of life
and loom she left so long ago behind.

From distant shores she brings back eyes
refracting an iridescence brighter
than the light she left.

The designs and dyes are different now,
the tension tauter on warp and woof
from all she saw in Marrakesh.

EVOLUTIONARY ARTIST

for Sylvia

Porcelain is the purest clay, kaolin decomposed
where it lay, gathering no alloy along the way,
fine as old wine, pliant, elegant—like her.

No dilettante, she knew she was an artist from
the age of eight, claimed her calling full-time
when time allowed, mentor to many then and now.

She traveled, taught, could not conceive a day
when the magic of her fingers would resist
rolling the tiny beads she was famous for.

After arthritis, she smiled, invented new ways
of rolling clay, forming scrolls compelling as
Qumran,
stacked in piles, gathered in baskets real as
gardens.

Over eighty now, her racing hands cannot keep
pace
with her laughing imagination, her evolving art,
curious as chromosomes, surprising as genes.

MENTOR

You will not know
the moment when
instead of seeking
you are sought.
And if you are,
you will not notice
because you yourself
will still be seeking,
seeing and sometimes
choosing the brambled
byways where lie
a lonely cistern,
cenotaph to souls
once lively there,
or strange new friend,
or poem that will
not let you go.

Maybe, only once or more
as you lean into a curve,
you will catch at the
periphery of your vision
a younger one watching you,
what it is you are looking for.

EVOLUTION

The oak is in the acorn, they say of trees,
but not of me, whose botany
assumes unprecedented lineaments
in the company of friends.

MOLLY

You lie in purple circled with pearls,
nearly empty of the ninety years you've earned.
Reaching among stringless beads of memory
for the names of your children,
you nevertheless greet guests
with a kindness that would be courtly
except for your accustomed modesty.

It is a modesty surely practiced,
for you had much to be modest for:
Sturdy stander-by of those who dared
to take forbidden seats where
anyone of lighter hue could eat;
Persistent rouser-up of those
who would not stand for anything;
Loved by many, feared by some
because you were afraid of none.

A visitor recalls a protest you directed
against one more fool reactor at Oak Ridge
twenty years ago when you were young.

"Yes," you say, "I seem to remember that.
We won, didn't we?" (It was a question.)
We did. And it was you who made it fun.

> (No size-eight social matron she,
> with rounded shoes and pointed pedigree,
> coiffed and clad in good gray wool,
> intently bent on doing good.

In her was quality far less tame,
the inborn power of some handsome beast
guarding the borders of the plain
with watchful eye and perfect ease.)

When was that splice of time for you—
were you thirty-seven? fifty-two?—
when for a moment all was bright:
children strong, parents well,
braced around by thriving kin,
and you were full of will and mind
to tackle wrong of every kind?

Were you wise enough in those fleet days
to savor color when you passed it by,
smiling with knowledge it would not last
and still was good and was a gift?

Surely you were then as you are now,
calmly responding when someone asks
if you are frustrated by all
that is fugitive from your recall.
"No," you say simply. "We all forget."

You continue:
"I sleep a great deal.
Fortunately I sleep easily.
I wake up, note the time,
then fall asleep again."

But later you add:
"Now there is nothing
I can give to anyone.
That is what I'm sorry for."

No.
Because you are here
in shape and form and name,
you summon stories from your guests
that offer recall to yourself.
That pleases you, you say.

What you do not see with your fine eyes
(the morning paper lies nearby)
is the good you do the storytellers,
whose best is leavened by what they tell.

That is the gift you give and will
until the moment you depart
(sooner than the hours feel
though not as soon as you may wish).

And then?
Then you will continue on
in memory authentic
as the pearls you wear.

LUSTRUM

His fifth Christmas and birthday gone
snapped shut like a spring-hinged trap
on a wide-eyed creature terrified
at her sudden incapacity.

Other anniversaries she had dreaded,
memorialized, raged against, smiled
a tear upon. The waves were settling.
Why was this December different?

The Romans knew the power of the lustrum,
a five-year span of measure so laden
they made for it a rite of purification
so life could right itself again.

I do not know the ways or reason
of their ministrations, only that I
flailed my loss this year wrought
tightly as a wounded animal caught.

How I saw "Angels in America," was flung
back to the time before the choice and chore
of living long instead of dying well,
could imagine nothing but your perfect death.

How our last journey took me away from
other loves, those closest that I chose,
husband first, and children, friends
who patiently waited through my grief.

How your last beloved Christmas Eve
I overcompensated, stayed with them
at the Cathedral service instead of being
home with you. What must you have thought?

How I was not patient with your partner at the end,
had loved him mostly for his love of you.
I think you loved but did not like him either then,
saw his wants surpass all else including you.

How I lost another brother the day
that I lost you, no longer trying
to make right what no one ever could
but we two had long committed to.

Now I have said the hard things.
Maybe it takes five years to say them,
maybe that is why this anniversary is so raw
I only now can cauterize the edges of recall.

RELENT

Lent is one long
Saturday before
Easter, dumb denial
of the awful death
by legal torture
of the day before.

How on that one day
at least could any
Christian rise in
righteous vindication
of the state's right still
to kill that way?

CORPUS CHRISTI

A town in Texas,
a gathering of the faithful,
the body of Christ, a McNally play.

My good brother and I
grew up in the wings
of all those worlds

played out on the stage that day
precisely thirty-five years after another
hate crime in a Dallas street.

Never before had I entered a theater
through metal detectors and guards
eyeing faces contorted with rage.

All right, you say, let's talk about it:
What if Jesus *wasn't* gay?
That's fine. It's only that

he could have been, or different skin,
or woman, if Incarnation means
that God came out as one of us.

The dissenters' greatest wrath,
if only they had had the wit
to dare come in and see the play,

would have been how happy were
the faces of those who lived within
His company that day.

LAMENT NOT WITHOUT ANGER
Confederate Cemetery, Franklin Tennessee

Unruly sons of Tennesseans
gone to Texas with hopes
longer than the Alamo
return to lie orderly
forever in Franklin.

Eternally kin with their cousins
side by side in stone rows
of cold camaraderie,
what did they think
why they died?

No matter. All now is moot,
save for their sister raging late
in the sullen dusk at all
their lively laughter
dashed to dust.

LINES UPON LOSING A JOURNAL

> Losing a passport is an inconvenience
> Losing a journal is a disaster
> —Robert Martins

Hurrying to leave the train at Pisa
I left behind the record of the weeks before
and grieved that with the record
all was lost.

Once I knew the small bound book was gone
    for good
after all efforts failed to find it, I worried
the absence like a child the space left by a
new-pulled tooth.

The dailiness, I knew, could be reconstructed
    according to the need.
The names alone of places stayed could serve
as suns governing by their gravity whole
circuits of stories:

Astoria Nomikos Galini Kalypso Olympic Victoria
Suisse Adua Bartoli Consoli di Mare Milano
    San Marco—
each a small lifetime compressed into syllables,
diamonds from coal.

But what of the dreams that graced each day with
color, raiment, shape—those thoughts that flocked
unbidden, metamorphosing slowly into meaning
as I watched?

How do I salvage those while the wind blows rain
hard against my pane in Castiglioncello
where finally I landed after a bleak diversion
through unlovely Livorno?

* * * * * *

How it felt to circle the Martinengo Bastion of old
Iraklion where Kazantzakis lies beneath a stone
    that reads
"I hope for nothing, I fear nothing, I am free" but
bears no name.

And how later in that dear narrow room in Rome
at 26 Piazza di Spagna, I wondered if Nikos
    knew what
clear-eyed Keats demanded, that a poet's name
    be writ
in water only.

How at that same door in '44 the soldier-poet of the
Second War, the one descended from Archilochus,
knocked to announce "I am a student" and
    rejoiced to
surrender to poetry.

How my room at the Nomikos Villa was a trapezoid
wedged into the core of the volcano, widening toward
the caldera of Santorini like a birth canal from the
center of earth.

How I felt when I saw Apollo holding the smiling
child
at Olympia, both of them coaxed (at what cost?)
out of marble from the mines at Paros I had
visited only
a day before.

How I came to see that the corridor from the high
plains
of Texas to just south of Taos, where the air is
composed
of the same humors as I am—old Epicurus believed
souls are matter—

skips like a stone over an ocean and several seas to
the flat high-skied Aegean where I feel the same
primeval
oneness that Parmenides said once was true of
all of us.

How Rome became at once so much more like home
and so much more remote from all my grasp
that I embraced her as I might
a furtive lover

whom I must flee before first light, before
first pealing of the bells all round
so not to be caught lying
with a stranger.

How Michelangelo's Last Judgment says no one thing
but how his Expulsion from the Garden does:
that the very knowledge that makes us human
 will also
break our hearts.

How I felt an uncontestable shifting of the poles
 from
Righting Wrong to Writing Plain, and how I
 wondered
which of these—or is it friends?—will matter
 most when
all is done.

How there were moments en route when I felt as
 if I were
living the story I'm writing as surely as a quilter
piecing the leftover fragments of multiple
lives into art.

How dearly I seek to convey all those characters
 lurking
in my brain like Michelangelo's prisoners
into a braille writ clear enough for all the
world to see.

How Florence in June at least has imploded
with so vast a horde of earnest weary tourists
that the scholars, painters, master builders of
all her art

would scatter in panic if they knew,
leaving only the Medici capitalists
to make from all the consumers
one last florin.

How Michelangelo knew what Vergil knew, what so
few do,
that it is possible, but only by the finest hew,
to tell the truth and please
the patron too.

How Brunelleschi's double dome is a metaphor
not for a city only but for life, the one enclosing
the vast unknown within, the other, that without,
and how we,

like his laborers, traverse the narrow catwalks
between
the two, their curves dizzying us always bending over,
with nothing at a distance we can see
to steady us,

until, pausing in the endless work to steal
a bite or kiss, we catch through tiny windows
a shining glimpse of the vast round plate below or
azure bowl above

and know then that the work is good, even if
we must soon descend the tiny curl of steps down
toward the door that exits to or from the world in
one direction only.

How I asked myself then if I had accomplished
enough,
become whatever inchoate thing I once aspired
to be,
then heard as surely as if spoken to, Do the work,
the
rest will follow.

How the end and beginning of stories are always lies
because both deny the thousand-stranded skein
that always ends later
and begins before

but how even this cannot divert a heart from a
journey
or a poem until at last, as Rodin said of any art,
each must be abandoned but
is never finished.

HAIKU

Lovers first
they bowed and began
the long slow dance of friends
to the last.

PENELOPE RETURNING

Alone on the shore of Ithaca, Penelope sat
absorbed in the shimmer of the dusk-bronzed sea,
searching for ways to tell what happened
after Odysseus came home at last.

Once he had powered his way into
his rightful place with his great bow,
she loosed the string of hers,
her vigil done, her only child now launched

beyond the reach of his mother's kind eyes
hiding the worries that circled her counsel
throughout his life, the two decades she
leaned toward him with all her weight and wit.

She conceived her plan a year after Odysseus's
    return,
waited patiently until the time was right.
Mentes arrived to rest his merchant crew,
take provisions, visit Ithaca for the night.

In early morning upon their olive bed
she turned quietly to Odysseus and said:
"I'll go to Egypt now. I've always wanted to.
Mentes will take me. I'll be safe, I know."

Her husband swung his gaze toward her,
mind churning with all the habits of manhood
the world and his birth had prescribed,
once again caught by the force of her courage.

Odysseus had loved her first for her beauty,
hard thereafter for her far-arching heart,
soon upon that for her lively competence,
the gift that promises a partnership for life.

"Yes," he nodded, "of course." He knew his wife.
In the day she gathered what she needed
for the journey, then put half of it away.
Half her joy the thought of traveling light.

She prepared a feast for the evening meal,
embraced the household, turned with a heavy heart
and lightness of step to board the craft
that would give to her the world.

As they rounded the western shoals
of Cephalonia she began to comprehend
what she had done. Demons of doubt
raised their frenzied whirl around her.

Guilt eroded her resolve as she wept
inconsolably, salt tears mixed with spray
at the stern where she fixed her eyes back
toward the home she left with such apparent ease.

She cried without trying to stop, only later
identifying guilt as the first monster
she must face and overcome. Others loomed
as soon as she pondered all she left behind:

How would father and son get along in her absence,
still new to each other and so little together,
son learning to become a man at the same time
Odysseus at last was learning to father?

Would they eat meals at tables
laced with thought and conversation,
or merely feed their hunger grazing
as they passed the cooking fires?

A serving girl, Melantho's daughter,
shifty-eyed and waitful, watched her depart;
Penelope saw her calculating her chances
with the master while the mistress was away.

Then, as the ship split the gentling waves
into the open sea, a moment came, still
as a hummingbird suspended, when she felt
duty fade and the joy of solitude encircle her

like the lifting light shining around
a well-loved child in love with life,
but burnished now far brighter by all
she knew from all the living she had earned.

Turning confident toward the bow, she did not
again look back. She reached Egypt,
climbed the pyramids as she had dreamed,
ate alone at dusk, made strange new friends.

No suitors waited slaying on her arrival home,
for she had razed hers one by one upon the road.
Like a sphinx, she left their leers in the markets
leveled with lances from her steely gaze.

With one like-minded journeyer she shared a meal;
every story sparked another, flint for one another's
steel.
They parted with regret, braced only by guessing
how great the love at home that taught each how to
love.

Still he is lodged in her heart's estate
that no heir will ever know,
nor gaggle of glaring shrews who confuse
their envy with their rectitude.

She is home. To most she seems the same,
though the sun's magic has settled on her skin,
her hair gleams free as a dancing child's,
turquoise eyes ashine with something new.

For a while she is strangely lonely,
chooses selectively the duties she resumes,
finds it hard to become host of her own home again
after being so long a guest of the world.

She delights to give the gleaming gifts
chosen so carefully for her beloveds,
sorrowing only that she must meter the density
of detail of how she came upon each prize.

She rises, returns to the hearth of her heart's desire,
knows at last that Ithaca is not the journey
but the stenography of stories
to make the journey known.

ACKNOWLEDGMENTS

"For John," "Mrs. Wilson," and "Easter Poem II" originally appeared in *Seasons of Grief and Grace* (Nashville and London: Vanderbilt University Press, 1994); "Mentor," "Evolution," and "Molly" originally appeared in *Athena's Disguises: Mentors in Everyday Life* (Louisville: Westminster John Knox Press, 1998). "Molly" appeared also in the *Tennessean*, March 24, 1996, 5D. "Evolutionary Artist" appeared in *number: an independent journal of the visual arts* #38 (summer, 2000) 26.